More Assemblies for Young People

ANTHONY BULLEN

MAYHEW-McCRIMMON
Great Wakering

First published in Great Britain in 1979 by
MAYHEW-McCRIMMON LTD.
Great Wakering Essex England

© Copyright 1979 by Anthony Bullen

ISBN 0 85597 282 3

Edited by Robert B Kelly
Printed by Mayhew-McCrimmon Printers Ltd

CONTENTS

Introduction 5

Getting to know you 6

Making friends 8

Food 10

Children who are sick 12

Brothers and sisters 14

Space flight 16

From sadness to joy 18

Honesty 20

Mothers 22

Forgiving people 24

People are precious 26

Sharing 28

The Lord's Prayer 30

Deaf people 32

On listening 34

Homes 36

Mr. Amen 38

Being afraid 40

Pets 42

Goodbye till then 43

INTRODUCTION

The previous volume, *TWENTY-FOUR ASSEMBLIES FOR JUNIORS* has been through several reprints and it seemed that the time was ripe for a follow-up. I offer this second collection of suggestions for Assemblies, as I did the first, with some reservation. For one thing, it would be far better for the pupils themselves, in collaboration with the class teacher, to build up the assembly, choosing their own readings, songs, illustrations and stories. Better that by far than that they should be presented with a ready-made assembly, created by someone unfamiliar with their background, ability and needs. For another thing, if a number of assemblies has but a single author, inevitably there must be a certain sameness about them.

However, it seems that the appetite of teachers for Assembly material is insatiable and so, having declared my reservations about the value of pre-fabricated assemblies, may I add the following suggestions for the use of this second series:

* The teacher is asked to use the material as a guide only. Simply to offer the Assemblies to the children as they stand would probably result in a lifeless presentation. The ideas need to be mulled over by the children, additions and deletions made according to the particular demands of the school.

* The children must be firmly led into making spontaneous suggestions.

* Ideally, no Assembly should last longer than fifteen minutes. Far better for the children, at the end of the Assembly, to wish it had lasted longer than to be conscious of its length.

* It would be ideal, also, if pleasant recorded music could be played before and after.

* One needs to avoid the over-spectacular. And any sense of rivalry between one class and another is to be eschewed. Simplicity and humble reverence should be the key notes.

* Above all it is important always to keep the objective of any Assembly constantly in mind: a reverent, enjoyable turning to God, the loving Father, by the members of a united community, about things that concern and interest the members.

The impression one receives from current publications is that teachers are beginning to doubt the effectiveness of Assembly. This may perhaps be more likely true of schools where the pupils come from a variety of religious or non-religious backgrounds and members of the Staff themselves hold widely differing attitudes towards the value of school worship. However, I still believe that where a majority of the children come from homes where the Christian Faith is actively desired by parents for their children, and where most members of Staff are convinced of the value of Christian worship, an interesting and enjoyable Assembly can be a major formative influence on the child's relationship with God and with his peers.

Anthony Bullen,
St. Paul's,
West Derby,
Liverpool.

GETTING TO KNOW YOU

This might be the first formal Assembly of the School Year. It will be an opportunity for Top Juniors to be given a taste of responsibility for leadership throughout the school. Present at this Assembly will be timid children feeling lost and homesick.

An invitation from the class presenting the Assembly might be sent to the caretaker, secretary, dinner ladies, traffic warden. Of course, all the teachers in the school should be present and visible.

Leader 1:   This morning we want to give a big welcome to anyone who is new to the school.

(Mention might here be made of the pupils of First Juniors, any new members of Staff, new helpers, etc.)

We all find it strange when we go to a new place for the first time. Sometimes we feel shy and we don't want to speak to anyone in case we look silly. But in this school we all want to be friends.

Leader 2:   We want no one to feel strange or shy. So let's begin by singing a song together. We are all children of God, and that means we are brothers and sisters of Jesus whose life we share. And so the first thing we do together is to sing our praise in honour of Jesus Christ.

Song: *Praise him* [CH 259] (3 verses)

Headteacher: I should like to welcome to the school . . .

(Here, the Headteacher might briefly introduce the new faces to the rest of the school.)

I should like these newcomers to know that we are very glad they have joined our community. The important part of the word 'community' is this —

*(A pupil might hold up a card on which is written in bold letters the word **UNITY**.)*

Unity means UNITED. And that means that we try and work together.

Let us pray.

(Pause)

Heavenly Father,
we are your children
and brothers and sisters of Jesus Christ.
Keep us in the year ahead a united family,
working well together and playing well together.
We make this prayer through Jesus Christ, our Lord.
Amen.

(Pause)

The response to the prayers we are going to say is this:
Keep us all united, Lord.
(Various children should say the following petitions):
When we are tempted not to bother about each other . . .
Keep us all united, Lord.
When we work and when we play . . .
Keep us all united, Lord.
On the playground and in the classroom . . .
Keep us all united, Lord.
Boys and girls, young and older . . .
Keep us all united, Lord.

Headteacher: And now we say slowly together the prayer which unites all Christians,
(and as we do so we join hands in a large circle).
Our Father . . .

Final song: *Praise him* [CH 259] (verses 4 & 5)

MAKING FRIENDS

Some of the children will have prepared for this Assembly by writing a few sentences on 'Friends'. 'Why I like to have a friend.' 'What can my friend expect from me?' 'How we became friends.' 'How we fell out of friends.'

Leader 1: This morning we are going to think and pray about 'friends'. Some of our class have written about friends and they are going to read what they have written.

Leader 2: Now we are going to perform a little play in which we show how two people became close friends of Jesus.

(Children mime according to the text.)

Narrator: John the Baptist was busy baptizing people in the river Jordan. When John came up out of the water, he suddenly pointed to someone who was walking by and said:

John: Look, there is the lamb of God. There is God's chosen leader.

Narrator: Two of John's followers began to walk after Jesus along the river bank. After a few yards Jesus turned round.

Jesus: What is it you want?

Andrew: Where do you live, Master?

John: Yes, Master, show us where you live.

Jesus: Come and see.

(They move off and sit down together.)

Narrator: And they stayed with him all day and became close friends.

Leader 1: Those two friends later died for Jesus. Jesus had said:

Jesus: Greater love than this no one has than that he lays down his life for his friends.

Leader 2: We will pray that we will try to help our friends and not just use them for what we can get out of them.
Heavenly Father,
it is your Holy Spirit who gives us the power to stay true to our friends.
Through this Holy Spirit
may we try to help our friends and not try to use them.
Amen.

Leader 1: Now we thank God our Father for giving us Jesus to be our Friend. We can't see him but we believe he is with us because he said:

Jesus: Where two or three are gathered together in my name, I am there with them.

Leader 1: And so he will be with us now. Wherever we go, he goes with us. We

8

can talk to him and he listens to us.

Final Song: *Kum ba yah, my Lord (Come by here)* [CH 162]
or
Where would we be without Christ our Lord [CH 359]

FOOD

It might help if either the song of *Food, Glorious Food* (from *Oliver*) could be played or sung. The background to the song, (Oliver in the boys' home daring to ask for 'more') explained. This would be an interesting start to the Assembly, but could be dispensed with.

The point of this Assembly is to help the children appreciate how fortunate they are to have three square meals a day, when about a quarter of the world's children go to bed hungry each night. An appreciation of their good fortune should lead them

      (1) to thank God;

      (2) to avoid wasting food;

      (3) to do something for those less fortunate in other lands.

(Cook and the dinner-ladies might be invited, if the Assembly takes place after the morning break.)

Leader 1: This morning we are going to think and pray about food. Some of our class wrote about which food they liked most and which food they didn't like. This is what they wrote:

      (Six or seven children read their pieces out. For example:

      'I love to hear the bacon cooking in the frying pan, and the lovely smell. It's the best meal of all.'

      'When I was little I liked jellies but now I would rather have toasted cheese.')

Leader 2: Sometimes in our school it happens that a lot of good food gets wasted. This is because some children eat sweets or crisps just before dinner and so they are not hungry when the dinner is put before them.

Leader 3: But our mothers and fathers pay a lot for our school dinners and our bodies need the vitamins and the nourishment of proper meals and so we should try not to waste any food.

Leader 1: We are going to say three prayers.

(John) will say the first prayer and it will be to thank God for giving us food.

Child 1: Heavenly Father,

we want to thank you for the food we eat

and for the enjoyment we get from eating our food.

We thank you for our mothers and fathers

who work so that they can pay for the food which keeps us alive.

We also thank you for those who cook our food and give it out.

Amen.

Leader 2:	And now (Mary) is going to say a prayer about not wasting food.
Child 2:	Heavenly Father, sometimes we are faddy and we say we don't want to eat things even though we know the food will make us strong and well. When we are tempted just to push the food to the side of our plates and not eat any more, we will try to think of children in other lands who are very hungry. **Amen.**
Leader 3:	And now a prayer from (Jimmy) so that we will be generous with our pocket money.
Child 3:	Father, some children never get enough to eat. We have more than we need. We will try to be generous and, if we get the chance, we will give some of our pocket money to help farmers in other lands grow more food. We make these three prayers through Jesus Christ, our Lord. **Amen.**
Leader 1:	And now we will sing together a thank-you song for our meals: *Thank you* [CH 298]
Final song:	Thank you for our eggs and bacon, thank you for sausages and chips, thank you for everything that's tasty, passing through our lips. Thank you for all the sweets and jellies, thank you for the ice cream treat, thank you for all the food you give us, and for all we eat. Thank you to the dinner ladies, thank you to the Head Cook, too. Thank you to all the Staff who work here, and to you 'Thank You'.

CHILDREN WHO ARE SICK

Leader: Here is a letter from a child who was taken into hospital. It was a big hospital in the North of England, just for children.

Reader 1: 'I came into this hospital a week ago. I had been having sore throats a lot and the doctor said I ought to have my tonsils out. I was put into a ward with a lot of other children who were all waiting for operations. Some were only very little and cried when their mothers left them. The nurses were very nice. One of them gave me a jig-saw to do while I was waiting to be prepared for my operation.
After the operation it was hard to swallow but it didn't hurt much. The doctor said I wouldn't catch so many colds. The hospital is very big. There is one ward for children with broken legs or arms, or bad backs. This is another ward for children with blood disorders. Another ward is called 'Intensive Care Unit' for children who have been in accidents. They have all sorts of machines to keep people alive, even though they are very seriously ill. One girl was brought in months ago after being knocked down by a motorbike. She was unconscious for weeks. Her mum and dad and brothers and sisters came in often to see her. They talked to her a lot and only the other day did she start to reply.
I know one thing; when I come out of hospital, I shall be more often thanking God for my health.'

Reader 2: Not all sick children are in hospital. Sometimes children are not well in school. They get headaches, tummy-aches, they fall and cut themselves or get hurt at football or rounders. When this happens, we should try to be kind.

Reader 3: Jesus said 'Do to others what you would want them to do to you.' If we are sick, we want children to be nice to us. If others are sick, we must be nice to them. Let us pray now for sick children and the doctors and nurses who look after them.

Child 1: For the doctors and nurses in the hospitals of our town.
(Pause)
Lord, in your mercy . . .
. . . **hear our prayer.**

Child 2: For the children who are in hospital in our town.
(Pause)
Lord, in your mercy . . .
. . . **hear our prayer.**

Child 3: For the children who are sick at home and wonder if they are ever going to get better.
(Pause)

	Lord, in your mercy . . .
	. . . hear our prayer.
Child 4:	For the children of our school who are not well now . . .
	(These might be mentioned by name.)
	(Pause)
	Lord, in your mercy . . .
	. . . hear our prayer.
Reader 4:	Let's do three things in our prayer:
	remember to thank God for our health;
	be kind to those who are sick;
	be brave when we are not well.
	Dear God our Father,
	we thank you for our good health.
	We are sorry for those who are not well
	and we will try to be especially kind to them.
	If we should be sick,
	we will try not to make a big fuss,
	we will try to be brave,
	just as your Son Jesus was when he suffered for us.
	We will try to trust you,
	and keep on believing that we are in your hands.
Final song:	*He's got the whole word in his hands* [CH 117] (alternative 'He's got sick children in his hands')

BROTHERS AND SISTERS

Most young brothers and sisters in most families spend most of their time quarrelling. In this Assembly we ask the children to look squarely at their own families and ask, if quarrelling is so prevalent, why it should be, and then decide on some action about which they might then pray.

Leader 1: Today we are going to think and pray about quarrels in a family. In many families brothers and sisters quarrel quite a lot. Just listen to this part of a cassette which some members of our class made up:
'Take your hands off that "Action Man" — it's mine.'
'Dad says you've never got to play with my things ever again.'
'I want (Star Trek). If you don't want to watch it, you can go outside.'
'But I don't want crisps. I want sweets.'
'Stop messing about with my things.'
'I'll never speak to you again.'
'It's not my turn to dry the dishes — it's yours.'
'I want to put my records on and I don't want to hear yours.'

Have you heard that sort of a conversation in your house? It can make things unpleasant.

Leader 2: Why do children in a family quarrel so much?

Child 1: Because they want their own way and won't give in.

Child 2: Sometimes because they are jealous of each other.

Child 3: Because they're always saying 'This is **mine**'.

Child 4: Because they are frightened they will get pushed out.

Leader 1: Families should be happy and could be happy. Listen to this message from the Gospel.

Narrator: The friends of Jesus were arguing as they walked along the road. They were arguing about who was going to be the most important when Jesus set up his Kingdom. When they got to the end of the journey, Jesus said to them:

Jesus: What was it you were arguing about as we walked along the way?

Narrator: But they were silent, because they were ashamed and Jesus said to them:

Jesus: You mustn't try to lord it over each other. You must try to serve each other just as I have served you.

Narrator: And at the end of his life Jesus gave his friends an example. Before the last supper he tied a towel round his waist and went from one to another, kneeling before each of them and washing their feet. He was doing the job which only slaves did.

Leader 2:	So let's pray for our families that we will live at peace with each other.
	(Pause)
	Heavenly Father,
	we ask you to send your Holy Spirit to each of our families
	so that brothers and sisters will try not to be nasty to each other
	but will try hard to live happily together,
	sharing their things and helping each other.
	We make this prayer through Jesus Christ, our Lord.
	Amen.
Leader 1:	The response to each of those petitions is:
	Lord, give us peace.
Child 5:	When we feel angry with our brothers or sisters . . .
	. . . Lord, give us peace.
Child 6:	When we are just about to start having a row . . .
	. . . Lord, give us peace.
Child 7:	When our younger brothers and sisters spoil our games . . .
	. . Lord, give us peace.
Child 8:	When our older brothers and sisters push us around . . .
	. . . Lord, give us peace.
Leader 1:	And now let us turn and give each other the handshake of peace — saying as we do — 'Peace be with you'.
Final song:	*Peace, perfect peace* [CH 257]

SPACE FLIGHT

We can use the children's natural interest in space flight to help them appreciate something of the greatness of God, in face of which we get a feeling of awe, a necessary prelude to the prayer of adoration.

The psalm will need to be copied out by the children.

Leader 1: Have you ever wondered what it must feel like to sit strapped in position in a spaceship waiting for that first frightening moment when the count-down starts?

(The following commands might have been tape-recorded beforehand or else another child could read them out.)

'All systems go.'

'Gantries away.'

'Thirty seconds to lift off.'

'We have ignition.'

'10 . . . 9 . . . 8 . . . 7 . . . 6 . . . 5 . . . 4 . . . 3 . . . 2 . . . 1 . . . ZERO.'

Imagine the feeling of the astronauts as they break into silence through the sound barrier, the noise of their rockets left behind.

Leader 2: Then they see the earth being left behind too and they are on the way to the stars. Some of the stars would take millions of years to reach. There are a 1,000 million stars in our galaxy and a thousand more galaxies in the Universe.

Leader 3: When the first astronauts were flying round the moon one of them took the Bible, God's Book, and he read this passage for all of us on earth to hear. This is what he read: 'In the beginning, God created the universe'. The great universe has come from God who made it all without any difficulty.

Leader 4: And yet even though the universe is far bigger than we can imagine, it is not as important as a single human. Any one person in this classroom is greater than all the stars put together.

Leader 5: When Jesus was little he learnt prayers by heart at his mother's knee. The prayers were called psalms and we are all going to say one now. We are going to say it like monks say it — with one half of the room saying one half and the other half of the room saying the other half. It is Psalm 8.

Left-hand side: **O Lord our God, we can see your greatness in all the world.**
Your glory is in the skies.
Your glory is sung by children and little ones.

Right-hand side: **When I look at the sky which you made**
at the moon and the stars which you set in their places

why should you bother to think of us?
we are so small and yet you care for us.

Left-hand side:Yet men and women are only just a little less great than you are,
because you think people are wonderful.
You have put people in charge of the world
so that they have control of everything.

Both together: Glory be to the Father,
and to the Son,
and to the Holy Spirit.
As it was in the beginning,
is now,
and ever shall be,
world without end.
Amen.

(Pause)

Leader 5: When some people of another religion want to show God that they worship him, they kneel down and bow low so that their forehands touch the floor. We are going to do that now.

(Children kneel.)

Now that we are all kneeling, please say after me.
O God, you are great, you are good.
O God, you are great, you are good.
We adore you.
We adore you.
Now we bend forward and touch our foreheads on the ground.

Final song: *Oh Lord, my God* [CH 227]

FROM SADNESS TO JOY (A Resurrection Assembly)

Leader 1: There was a film on TV a few years ago called *The Railway Children*. It told the story of those three young children whose father disappeared. The children didn't know why but, in fact, the father was wrongly accused of stealing and was put in prison. Mother had to bring the children up on her own and she moved to a little house in the country. It was near a railway and the children used to love watching the steam trains chugging past. One day the eldest girl got a hint that if she went to the railway station to meet the stopping train from London she might get a wonderful surprise. She hoped against hope that it might be her father come back again.

Leader 2: The train stopped in the station and a number of people got off. But no one even a little bit like her father appeared. The girl began to feel very sad. Still more when the guard blew his whistle and the train began to move off with great clouds of steam.

Tears came to her eyes. Tears of sadness as she began to think all her hopes had gone. Then through the steam and fog she saw a figure, the figure of a man. Could it be him? The steam and smoke cleared away and he was clearly visible. It was her dad. She rushed to him. They put their arms around each other. Her tears of sadness turned to tears of joy.

Leader 3: Listen now to this piece of the Gospel story. The same sort of thing happens. Jesus has died on the cross. His friends think all their hope has gone. One of his friends, Mary Magdalen, came to the tomb on the Sunday morning.

Mary: This is where they laid the body, in this vault. They rolled a great stone against the entrance.
(Surprised)
But the stone has gone. I must look in to see what's happened to his body.
But it's not there.
His body has gone.
Someone must have taken it.
There's a man over there. He must be the gardener.
I shall ask him if he knows anything.
'Sir, I have come to pray by the body of my friend, Jesus. But the body has gone. Can you tell me where they have put him?'

Jesus: Mary!

Mary: Master, it's you! It's really you! I thought you were dead for ever. But now you are alive again with a new life.

18

Jesus: Mary, go and tell all the others the good news that I am alive and I shall never leave them again.

Leader 1: Let's be quiet just for a moment and talk to our friend and brother, Jesus Christ, in our own words. We cannot see him but we believe he is with us. He said 'Where two or three are gathered together, I am there in the midst of them.'
(Pause for a moment.)
And now we will sing together:

Final song: *Alleluia, Sing to Jesus* [CH 7]
(It might help to explain that the word 'Alleluia' means 'Praise to God'.)

HONESTY

Narrator: Zacchaeus was a tax collector. He went round taking money from people for the Government. Nobody likes to have money taken from them and so Zacchaeus was very much disliked. Our class are now going to do a play about Zacchaeus and what happened to him one day when he met Jesus.

(Six or seven children stand in line with their backs to the rest of the children)

Crowd voices: Jesus is coming along here any minute.

They say he's a wonderful person.

It's good to be in Jericho on a day like this.

Look he's coming. I can see the crowd around him.

Zacchaeus: *(Comes up behind the line)*
Oh dear! I can't see a thing.

Voices: There's that rotten tax collector behind us.

We mustn't let him see anything.

Tax collectors are scum.

Zacchaeus: I'm too small to see over their shoulders. I'll have to climb up this sycamore tree.
(Climbs on chair)
No one will see me here anyway.

Crowd: Here is Jesus.

Let's give him a clap.

(Children clap)

He's stopped walking.

Why's he looking up into that tree?

It's that dirty tax collector.

Mayor: Master, I'm the mayor of this town. You are very welcome. Don't stop here. Come to the town hall for tea.

Jesus: Zacchaeus, hurry on down from that tree. I'm coming to *your* house for tea.

Mayor: But, Master, he's a filthy dirty tax collector. He steals money from people.

Zacchaeus: Jesus, I'm very pleased to have you come to my house. And I promise you anything I've stolen I'll give it back.

Jesus: *(to the crowd)*
God is pleased with Zacchaeus today because he is promising to be honest.

Leader 1: Every now and again someone is tempted to take something that belongs to someone else. It might be money or sweets or a toy. If we want to remain friends of Jesus, we must say: 'No, that is not mine to take. I shall leave it.'

Leader 2: We will keep quiet for a moment and think of any times we have been dishonest and tell God in our hearts that we are sorry just as Zacchaeus told Jesus he was sorry.

(Pause)

Heavenly Father,

we are sorry for the times we have taken what did not belong to us.

If we have stolen, we will try to pay back.

May your Holy Spirit give us the strength not to give way to temptation.

MOTHERS

It shouldn't be difficult for the class in preparation for this Assembly to collect pictures of mothers from various magazines. They could paste them onto a long strip of paper which could be pinned up at the front of the Assembly Hall. Obviously, individual pictures won't be big enough to be clearly visible to everyone but some of the children could describe them. Interspersed through the pictures could be printed in bolder lettering such slogans as:

> **WE LOVE OUR MUMS**

> **MY MOTHER IS VERY SPECIAL**

> **NO ONE CAN TAKE MUM'S PLACE**

and so on. Some of the children could also bring pictures of their own mothers which they could briefly describe.

This part of the Assembly would be informal and spontaneous. The teacher might introduce the various children.

Leader 1: If you have a baby brother or sister aged about one-and-a-half or nearly two, you will know how exciting it is wondering when they are going to start talking. They make gurgling noises and they nearly seem to talk but you can't make much sense of what they say. When they do begin to talk, usually the first word they said is 'Mama'. And Mama is the most important person in anyone's life.

Leader 2: Here is a letter written by a boy whose mother went into hospital:
Dear Mum,
I hope you are soon better. We all miss you very much. Dad tries hard to look after us all but he doesn't do as well as you. Until you went into hospital, we didn't know just how much you do for us each day.

Leader 3: The response to each of these prayers is:
Father, in heaven, we thank you for our mothers.

For all the meals they cook for us . . .
Father, in heaven, we thank you for our mothers.

For the clothes they wash and iron for us . . .
Father, in heaven, we thank you for our mothers.
For the times they stay by us when we are sick . . .
Father, in heaven, we thank you for our mothers.
For the times they buy nice things for us . . .
Father, in heaven, we thank you for our mothers.

Leader 4:   Jesus, too was very fond of his mother. As he died, he asked his best friend, John, to look after her. We, too, should be fond of Mary who is not only Jesus's mother but ours as well. And so we end this Assembly by singing a song in her honour.

Final song: Children's favourite hymn to Our Lady.

FORGIVING PEOPLE*

Leader: This morning our class are going to act out a story which Jesus told. Jesus often answered people who put a question to him by telling a story. This is how we have the story of the servant who wouldn't forgive.

Peter: Lord, how many times have I got to forgive someone who has done me wrong? Our Jewish law says that I must forgive three times. But the fourth time a person injures me I can say, 'No, I won't forgive you any more'. Would you say that if I forgive seven times it would be enough?

Jesus: No, Peter. Seven times is not enough. But seventy times seven times.

Peter: *(amazed)*
Seventy times seven times! That's, let me see, 490 times!

Jesus: No, Peter, it means times without number. You must always forgive. Let me tell you a story. There was once a king . . .

King: *(to a servant)*
Bring my chief servant to me. I have found out that he owes me a lot of money.
(The chief servant is brought in.)
Look my man. Do you realize what you owe me? It comes to, let me see,
(he looks at his notebook)
nearly £5 million.

Servant: £5 million! But I can't possibly pay all that.

King: Well if you're not going to pay it, I shall have you put in gaol and your wife and children. And I'll sell your house and all you own.

Servant: Sir, please don't do that. Just be patient with me. I will pay you all in time.

King: Very well. I'll forgive you. I wouldn't want you to suffer. So I'll let you off scot-free.

Chief Servant: Sir, thank you very much. I'm most grateful.

Jesus: As this man leaves the King, he comes across another servant and this is what he said.

Chief Servant: Look here you! Come over here. I've got something to tell you. You owe me £5 and I want it immediately.

Second Servant: But sir, I haven't got it.

*The play in this Assembly is taken from **Gospel Plays for Young People**, by Anthony Bullen (Mayhew-McCrimmon, 1979).*

Chief Servant: *(Getting hold of him)*

If you don't pay me that £5, I'll have you put in gaol, you and your wife.

Second Servant: Just be patient with me and I'll pay you it all soon.

Chief Servant: No. I won't wait.
(To other bystanders)
Take this man away and throw him into prison.

Jesus: The other servants when they heard what had hapened were very upset. They went to the King.

The other servants when they heard what had happened were very upset. They went to the King.

Servants: We are all very upset.
Your chief servant wouldn't forgive someone who owed him some money. It wasn't very much.
He's had him put into prison.

King: *(angrily)*
Bring my chief servant to me!
(Chief servant brought in.)
You wicked servant! I forgave you and you owed me £5 million. Now I hear you wouldn't forgive the poor man who owed you £5. I had pity on you who owed me so much. Why didn't you have pity on the one who owed so little?

Jesus: That is the story. You must forgive others if you want God your Father to forgive you. If you forgive others their failings, your Heavenly Father will forgive you yours.

Leader: Think of the times when you find it hard to forgive. When someone kicks you at football, trips you at rounders, is nasty to you in class. Things like this happen to all of us every day and we feel like getting our own back. But if we are Christians we must forgive even those who hurt us.

PEOPLE ARE PRECIOUS

Leader: Here is a story about a marvellous machine made by a very clever professor. It was a wonderful computer. Not much bigger than a typewriter. It was the cleverest machine in the world. All you had to do was to ask it any question you wanted and it would type out the answer in seconds. You could ask it, for example, what speed the wind is blowing in Singapore at this moment, and it would tell you straight away. It could even tell you what was going to happen — 'What horse will win the Grand National in 1983?' and up would come the answer. But there was one draw-back. The professor who had invented it had lost the design. No one would ever be able to make another like it.

The professor was on a world tour demonstrating this machine. It was worth at least ten million pounds. He came to our town and a big crowd of people came to watch the demonstration in the Town Hall. Among them was Charlie, ten years of age and interested in machines. But it was a hot afternoon and the professor was very boring. In the end Charlie slipped away into a corner near the window and sat down under a grand piano where he wouldn't be spotted. He fell asleep.

He must have been asleep for hours because when he woke up the big room was empty and dark. He was alone in it with this priceless machine. Then he smelt smoke. There was a fire. He heard people shouting in the street. 'The Town Hall's on fire and that priceless machine is still in there in the big room.'

Then Charlie heard the fire engines' sirens. Nearer and nearer they came. He heard the fireman's ladder bang against the window-sill. By this time the flames were coming through the floorboards. The window was shattered and there at the top of the ladder was the fire brigade officer.

He saw Charlie and he saw the priceless machine with flames getting nearer to it. He didn't know what to do. He shouted down to the Captain. 'Captain, there's a boy here as well as the machine. I can't save them both. There isn't time. Which is it to be? The lad or the machine worth £10 million?'

A crowd had gathered down below. And they all shouted: 'Save the lad. Forget the machine. It's the boy who's important.'

The fireman took Charlie in his arms and he was down the ladder in no time. As he got to the bottom, the whole building collapsed and the machine was completely destroyed.

Leader 2:   That story shows how every human being is worth more than any machine. What price are you worth? What price would your mum put on you? You are priceless. Every boy and girl, every man and woman is priceless. And so we have to treat everyone we meet with great respect. Here is a prayer:

Father in heaven,
you know and love each one of us by name.
May we respect one another and care for one another.
We make our prayer through Jesus Christ, our Lord.
Amen.

Final Song: *He's got the whole world* [CH117]

SHARING

This Assembly is going to be about sharing. So it would make sense if the class preparing it were secretly to collect and buy enough biscuits for all at the Assembly. These would be given out during the Assembly as a practical demonstration of the theme.

Leader 1: What is the worst thing you would like to be called? Suppose you heard someone talking about you only they didn't know you were listening. They might say some nasty things about you. They might say — You're lazy, you're not a good sport, you're dirty, you've got a crooked mouth, you're no good at your lessons. You may not like to hear any of those things very much but I'm sure there's one thing you would hate to hear — if someone were to say about you that you were MEAN, really mean.

Leader 2: None of us likes a mean person — someone who won't share, who goes off on his own and won't let other people join in his good fortune. It's not easy to share. It comes natural to us to want to get the best place, to keep the best things for ourselves. If others are short and we have plenty, to guard what we have and not let others have any of it.

Leader 3: This is what happened in an infants' class. It was the teacher's birthday. She brought in some chocolate biscuits for the children. As she gave them out she said, 'Now don't start eating till everyone's got a biscuit.' Then she suddenly saw that she only had twenty biscuits and there were forty in the class. She said, 'What are we going to do? There are twenty children without biscuits?' Straight away those who had biscuits put their hands round them and held them tightly. It came naturally to them not to share. The teacher said, 'You wouldn't want these other children to go without. You couldn't enjoy your chocolate biscuits and see them eating nothing.' Slowly the twenty with biscuits snapped them and gave away half. They began to smile. At first it had hurt but then they were glad.

Leader 4: One day Jesus was in the countryside far from any shops. There was a big crowd of people with him. One of his friends came to him.

Apostle: Sir, these people have been with us all day and they have had nothing to eat. Send them away and tell them to get their own food.

Jesus: Philip, you live round here. Where can we get food for all those people?

Philip: Master, £50 wouldn't be enough to buy food for this crowd. But there's Andrew. He may have an idea.

Andrew: It's not much of an idea; but there's a lad here with a few loaves and fishes but that wouldn't feed all these people.

Jesus:	Get them all to sit down and you feed them. Just share the loaves and fishes with them.
Friends:	Sit down everybody. We're going to give you something to eat. *(The class can now distribute chocolate biscuits to everyone in the Hall)*
Leader 5:	That's the sort of thing Jesus did. He shared his power with everyone. We must do what we can to share what we have with those who do not have as much.
Final Song:	*Let us break bread together on our knees* [CH169]

THE LORD'S PRAYER

Leader: The Lord's Prayer, the 'Our Father', is the most famous prayer that's ever been said. Billions of Christians of all denominations have said this prayer. Roman Catholics, Anglicans, Methodists, Baptists, and many other different religions are united when they say this prayer. Non-Christians, that is people who may not believe that Jesus is the Son of God, also say this prayer. This morning we are going to have another look at it. This is the way Jesus came to give it to his friends. Peter the Apostle begins the conversation.

Peter: Where has Jesus gone to, Andrew? He seems to have disappeared. I've been looking for him everywhere.

Andrew: When he goes off on his own like this he usually likes to pray. You remember what he said — go off on your own sometimes and talk to God your Father secretly. That's what he'll be doing. He'll be talking to his Father. He loves to do that.

Peter: Look, there he is.
(He points to Jesus who is kneeling)
Isn't he still? He doesn't even know we are here.

Andrew: What do you think he is saying? I wish I could pray like that. When I pray, I just make a mess of it and I yawn and wish the prayers were over.

Peter: Let's ask him. He won't mind if we interrupt him.
(To Jesus)
Jesus, teach us to pray.

Jesus: This is how you can pray:
(very slowly indeed, with pauses between each petition)
Our Father,

who art in heaven,

hallowed by thy name.

Thy Kingdom come.

Thy will be done on earth, at it is in heaven.

Give us this day our daily bread,

and forgive us our trespasses,

as we forgive those who trespass against us,

and lead us not into temptation,

but deliver us from evil.

(For thine in the Kingdom, the power and the glory for ever and ever.

Amen.)

(This might be sung solo to Estelle White's setting [CH375b]
The prayer can then be said or sung again by all present. A group of children could
have been prepared beforehand to do appropriate actions in front of the Assembly
so that the rest of the children in the Hall can copy them. This has been tried and
found to be very easy and the actions explain the words better than any verbal
description.

Our Father, who art in heaven	*arms raised heavenwards*
hallowed by thy name.	*all bow low*
Thy Kingdom come. Thy will be done on earth, as it is in heaven.	*arms crossed over breast*
Give us this day our daily bread,	*hands held forward, palms facing up*
and forgive us our trespasses,	*strike the breast with closed hands*
as we forgive those who trespass against us,	*shake hands with the person standing next to you*
and lead us not into temptation, but deliver us from evil.	*both helds held before eyes, palms outwards*
For thine is the Kingdom . . .	*children all take each other by the hand to form a ring or a line*

DEAF PEOPLE

Leader 1: We can see. We can speak. We can touch. We can smell things. We can taste things. We can hear.
If you had to lose one of those senses which would you most want NOT to lose. Your sight? Your speech? Your smell? Your ability to touch things? Your taste? Your hearing?

Leader 2: Many people would say that a blind person is the most handicapped. When you see a blind person, you feel you want to help him right away. Blindness is certainly a very serious handicap, but blind people can be helped to overcome their handicap.

Leader 3: People who deal with the handicapped say that deafness is the hardest handicap. Children who have never heard any sounds don't know how to speak properly. Children who are deaf don't look at though they are handicapped and so people don't try to help them like they do the blind. Children who are deaf feel very cut off. Although they can see TV they can't follow what's happening.

Leader 4: Let's say a prayer for the deaf.
(This prayer could have been written large on a blackboard, or children could each have copies, so that all can say it together)
Heavenly Father,
we pray for those who are deaf.
We ask you to send them your Holy Spirit
who will comfort them for their handicap.
We pray for those who look after the deaf.
We ask that if we meet deaf people,
we will treat them kindly.

Leader 5: Now we will pause for a moment and listen very carefully for all the sounds we can hear.
(Children may care to say what sounds they have heard during the silence)
And now let us thank and praise God for all the beautiful things we can hear.
(Various children can lead the following petitions. The response could be on a flash-card and held aloft)
For the sound of music which we love to hear . . .
. . . Lord God, we praise and thank you.
For the sweet singing of birds which we love to hear . . .
. . . Lord God, we praise and thank you.
For the sound of chips sizzling in the chip pan which we love to hear . . .

. . . Lord God, we praise and thank you.

For the sound of our mother's and father's voices which we love to hear . . .

. . . Lord God, we praise and thank you.

For the sound of the wind at night whistling round the house which we love to hear . . .

. . . Lord God, we praise and thank you.

(Children may have suggested other sounds.)

Leader 6:   Let us pray:
Heavenly Father,
we are very grateful to you for giving us our hearing.
We will try and use this gift of yours well
so that we will try to listen only to what is good,
what is beautiful,
what is true.
We make this prayer through Jesus Christ, our Lord.
Amen.

Final song: *Oh the love* [CH231]
(The next Assembly 'ON LISTENING' would follow naturally.)

ON LISTENING

The children in preparation for this Assembly could draw two very large ears and one large mouth, which might be cut out and pinned up in front of the assembled pupils. The children might be provided with paper and pencil and can sit on the floor.

Leader 1: In our last assembly we thought and prayed about deaf peole. Well there are probably no deaf people in this room. But there are plenty of people who never really *listen*. (John) is going to tell you a story and there are a lot of details in it. When he's finished, we'll see how well you have listened.

(John): The mountain is very high — 3,050 feet. It was a Thursday morning at 9 o'clock when we decided to climb it. There were five of us, three boys — John, Jim and Tony — and two girls — Mary and Jill. We each had sandwiches. I had ham and cheese. We climbed for an hour and a half and then we had a rest. Jill got cramp and decided not to climb any more but wait for us to come down. We got to the top at 1 o'clock, had our sandwiches and then came down.

Leader 1: Now here are the questions — see how well you listened:
— How high was the mountain?
— What weekday morning was it?
— What time was it when they decided to climb?
— What were the names of the boys, of the girls?
— What sort of sandwiches?
— How long did they climb?
— Who was ill? What was wrong with her?
— What time did they reach the top?
(The children might like to write their answers down.)
Who got them all right?
(Check)

Leader 2: We have drawn two very large ears and one mouth. God gave us two ears but only one mouth. So he expects us to listen twice as much as we speak. We must try and listen to each other.
While you listen you learn.
While you speak you are learning nothing.
While you listen you can be of help.

Leader 3: Here is a story from God's book, the Bible. It is about listening: Samuel was a young boy and he was a servant to Eli who was a minister in the temple. One night Samuel was lying on his bed. God called Samuel, 'Samuel! Samuel!' he said. Samuel thought it was Eli calling to him. So he woke Eli up and said, 'Master, what do you want?' Eli said 'I didn't call you, Samuel. Go back to bed.' So

34

Samuel went back to bed. Again God called to Samuel, 'Samuel! Samuel!' Once again Samuel thought Eli was calling him. So he woke Eli up and said 'Master, what do you want?' And Eli said, 'I didn't call you, Samuel. Go back to bed.' And it happened again, a third time. This time, Eli said, 'Samuel, it wasn't me who called you. It must have been God. Next time it happens, you must say, "Speak Lord, for your servant is listening".'

So Samuel went back to bed and God called Samuel again and Samuel answered 'Speak, Lord. Your servant is listening.' And God spoke to Samuel and told him what to do.

Leader 4: We are not going to hear God speak in the same way that you can hear me speak to you now. But he does speak in a secret way. He tells us what to do and how we ought to behave. So if you see another child in need of help, you stop and think. Maybe God is saying 'Go over to that child and help.' That is the way God speaks to us now.

Let us pray:
Heavenly Father,
you speak to us in all sorts of ways.
You speak to us through the beautiful world around us.
You speak to us through our friends,
our teachers,
our parents,
through the things that happen to us.
We promise that every day we will stop for a moment or two
and like Samuel say
'Speak, Lord, your servant is listening'.
We make this prayer through Jesus Christ, our Lord.
Amen.

Final song: *I watch the sunrise* [CH145]

35

HOMES

Leader 1: Today we are going to think and pray about homes, and how we feel safe at home. There's a big difference between a house and a home. A house is just bricks and mortar, windows and doors, slates and chimneys. But a home is a building in which people love and care for each other.

There or four children might now describe their homes. For example: 'We live at 63 Duke Street, it is a terraced house. There is my mum, my dad, big brother, big sister and a baby. We also have a cat called Susie. I don't like the winter much. But what I do like about winter is when we're all sitting together of an evening. My mum is usually knitting, sometimes ironing. My dad often falls asleep after he's had his tea. My big brother and sister are trying to get their homework finished. But we all feel close together.'

Leader 2: There have been a lot of songs about homes. Some of them are old songs.

(Could the children sing one or two of these old songs, like *Home Sweet Home, Keep the home fires burning.* Any modern songs about homes?)

Leader 3: A lot of stories have been written about homes as well. One of the most famous stories ever written was about a man called Odysseus. The whole story is about him trying to get home despite a lot of difficulties put in his way. The story only ends happily at the end of his journey when Odysseus arrives home and meets his family again.

Leader 4: The best two things about home are feeling safe and feeling wanted. We feel safe because we know we are loved by other members of the family even though at times we may quarrel a bit.

Leader 5: But in any home, if it is going to be happy everyone must put themselves out to help each other and be of service. This is the example Jesus gave us at his last supper with his friends.

(Five or six children are seated in chairs facing the Assembly. A child comes forward with a basin, puts a towel around his waist and goes to the first 'Apostle'.

Jesus: Peter, I'm going to wash your feet.

Peter: Wash my feet? But that's a slave's job. That's a job for servants. You will never wash my feet.

Jesus: If I can't wash your feet, we can't be friends.

Peter: In that case, Master, wash not only my feet but my head and my hands.

(Jesus goes to each of the 'Apostles' and acts as though washing their feet.)

Jesus: You see what I have done. You call me 'Master' and 'Lord' and that is what I am. If I, who am your Master, wash your feet, you must be prepared to do the same for each other.

Leader 6: So Jesus tells us we must do things for each other. Here is how we can help to make our homes happy:

Various children: Helping with the washing up;

cleaning our shoes ;

walking the dog;

tidying our bedrooms;

putting away our toys;

not arguing when mum says it's time for bed;

putting off the telly when we're told;

going messages.

Final Prayer: Lord Jesus,
you were once a child at home.
You helped your mother Mary about the house
and Joseph in his workshop.
May your Spirit live in us
and help us to make happy homes, too.

Final Hymn: *Come, Lord Jesus, come* [CH 51]

MR. AMEN

Leader 1: There was an old man in the parish. He was a retired engine-driver. He had silvery grey hair and ruddy cheeks and he was nearly always smiling. He lived on his own in a little cottage with green ivy climbing round the door and the two windows. He was often in church and the children used to call him 'Mr. Amen'. The reason they gave him this strange name was because when the priest ended the prayers with 'Through Jesus Christ, our Lord' or 'For ever and ever', before anyone else could say anything, this old man would always come out with a big 'Amen' in a loud voice.

Quite often as he came out of church people would stop him. 'I need a new washer on my tap', someone would say to him. Or, 'I can't shut one of my windows. Could you fix it?', or, 'The wire netting round the hen pen is loose and needs nailing back to stop the hens getting out'. To all these requests, usually made by old ladies who couldn't afford to pay, Mr. Amen always said 'Yes — I'll come today'. In fact 'yes' was Mr. Amen's favourite word.

Leader 2: And 'Yes' is really the meaning of Amen. It means — 'Yes, I agree'. It's something like 'Hear, hear' when people make speeches.

(The class will have been prepared to shout 'Hear, hear' after the following speech.)

Voice: 'What I say, ladies and gentlemen, is that the Government should give everyone ice-creams on Mondays, marsh-mallows on Tuesdays, caramels on Wednesdays, jellies on Thursdays and free trips in aeroplanes on Fridays.'

Class: 'Hear, hear.'

Leader 1: You see what it means. 'We agree.'

When we come to church, at the end of quite a lot of the prayers we say 'Amen'. There is one prayer at Mass which is called 'The Great Amen'. At a time not long after Jesus' resurrection, it was written down that Christians in their eucharist would really shout out a great Amen when the priest finished the prayer:

Voice: Through Jesus, with him, in him,
in the unity of the Holy Spirit,
all honour and glory is yours,
almighty Father,
for ever and ever.

Class: Amen.

Leader 2:   In some places this is sung to this melody:

Leader 3:   But we shouldn't just *say* Amen. We should *live* it. Just like Mr. Amen lived it out in his life. When we are asked to do things:

Various voices: 'Please may I join in your game? — **Yes.**
'Would you go on this message for mum?' — **Yes.**
'Will you clean your shoes?' — **Yes.**
'Will you read a story to your little sister?' — **Yes.**
'Will you turn the telly off and go to bed?' — **Yes.**
'Will you write a letter for granny's birthday?' — **Yes.**

It may not seem as though God is asking you to do things but very often it is he who is asking through other people. Jesus answered 'Yes' when God asked him to do things. 'With Jesus it was always "Yes" '. *(2 Corinthians 2:18)*

Voices: Jesus, will you come and heal my daughter? — **Yes.**
Jesus, will you feed the crowd? — **Yes.**
Jesus, will you bless these children? — **Yes.**
Jesus, will you carry this cross? — **Yes.**
Jesus, will you give yourself for all men and women? — **Yes.**

Leader 3:   That is how it should be with us.

Final song: *Amen! (as above)*
[Accompaniment CH 375a: transposed to 'F' here, for recorders.]

39

BEING AFRAID

The preparation for this Assembly could take the form of the children in the class writing a few lines about things they are afraid of. Probably most children will think that adults have no fears. It would be good for the class teacher to tell them what he/she used to be afraid of as a child, and is still afraid of as an adult. It is therapeutic for children to admit to their fears.

Opening song: *Kum ba yah* (Come by here) [CH 162]

Leader 1:   There is probably no one in this world who is not afraid of something or someone. Even Muhammad Ali *(or the current world boxing champion)* is afraid of something. The champion all-in wrestler in 1977 was scared of flying and would never get into an aeroplane. In our class, we prepared for this Assembly by writing about some of the things we are afraid of.

(The following are fairly typical.)

Child 1:   I am afraid of the dentist. I don't like the prick of the needle as he gives me the injection. But if I don't have an injection, I am afraid of the pain and the noise of the drill.

Child 2:   I'm afraid of mice and rats. I saw a mouse in our back kitchen the other day and I screamed. One day I saw a dead rat in our road, and it made me feel terrible.

Child 3:   I'm afraid of the dark. When my mum switches the light out in my bedroom at night, I ask her to leave the door open and the landing light on.

Child 4:   I'm afraid of swimming. I went to the baths with my dad, but I daren't go out of my depth into deep water. He held me up in the deep end but I was very frightened. I don't want to go again.

Leader 2:   Many Africans today are afraid of the sea. And the Jews in Jesus' time were more afraid of the sea than of anything else. When they thought of the sea they were reminded of dying. That is why the writers of the Gospels include the story of Jesus walking on the water of the Sea of Galilee to show that Jesus had overcome the power of death. This is what happened in the boat:

(Six children can pretend to be rowing.
A seventh child is Peter in charge.)

Peter: There's a nasty storm blowing up. The waves are getting bigger.

1st Apostle: I'm beginning to feel frightened.

Peter: Just keep rowing. If you let the boat go sideways to the wind, we will turn over and all be drowned.

2nd Apostle: It's getting worse. I think we are all going to drown.

3rd Apostle:	Look, there's a ghost!
4th Apostle:	Where? As though things aren't bad enough.
5th Apostle:	He's right. It's a ghost walking across the waves to us.
6th Apostle:	I don't think it's a ghost. I think it's Jesus.
Peter:	It *is* Jesus. At least I think it is. I'll call out to him.
	Jesus, if it is you, tell me to come to you across the water.
Jesus:	It is I. Don't be afraid. Yes, Peter, come to me.
Peter:	*(Peter gets out of the 'boat' and then he begins to sink.)*
	Lord, save me or I'll die.
Jesus:	*(Jesus helps him into the 'boat').*
	Have faith in me. I can help you overcome all your fears.
Leader 3:	But although Jesus was able to help others overcome their fears, a time came when he was frightened. It was the night before he died. He knew that it was going to be painful and he prayed.
Jesus' voice:	Father, if it is possible, take this suffering away from me. Yet not what I want; what you want.
Leader 3:	Let us pray.
	Lord Jesus Christ,
	we are sometimes frightened.
	But we know that since you overcame your fear
	and after dying you rose to new life,
	you are by our side wherever we go.
	We put our trust in you,
	our Friend, our Brother, our Saviour.
Final song:	*Christ be beside me* [CH 41]
	If the Assembly takes place in late afternoon:
	Day is done [CH 59]

PETS (In April or May)

The children who have pets might write about them: what they are, their names, why they have given them the name, anything interesting about them. On the lines of:

'We have a cat. We call him Sooty because he is absolutely black. He's sometimes in trouble because he digs his claws in the furniture. And we also worry sometimes about him catching birds. But he's a nice cat and he likes to be stroked. We give him one meal a day of Whiskas.'

'Our dog is a mongrel. We call him Patch because he has a black eye. He's a good house dog. If anyone touches the gate, he hears it and starts barking. He nearly got run over last week.'

Leader 1: When the world came into being, God gave men and women control over the animals. They were to give the animals names. But God wanted men to look after the animals who depend on us. If we left our pets, they couldn't look after themselves.

Leader 2: Every year at Christmas time, people buy pets for their children. Soon after Christmas there are a lot of stray dogs and stray cats roaming the streets. It's because some of the children have got tired of them, or won't look after them. And so the poor animals are just turned out. This is very cruel.

Leader 3: So let's promise God who gave us pets for our pleasure that we will look after them. Take them walks or play with them. See they get the right food. There are some animals too that are not pets and we must see that they are not harmed. At this time of the year birds are making nests. We should not disturb them or frighten them. They should be left to bring up their young in peace. It is very cruel to steal eggs out of nests.

Leader 4: Jesus must have been fond of animals because he spoke about them quite a lot. He talked of sparrows. He said:

Voice of Jesus: Not a sparrow dies but your Father knows about it.

Leader 4: He talked of hens and chickens, foxes and fish. And at his birth, it could be that cows and sheep were near him.

Leader 5: And now we will say a prayer:
Heavenly Father,
you have given us animals and pets for our enjoyment.
They depend on us to look after them and care for them.
We promise today to do all we can to see that they are well treated.
We make this prayer through Jesus Christ, our Lord.
Amen.

Final Song: *All things bright and beautiful* [CH 13]

GOODBYE TILL THEN

In preparation the children might think of 'goodbye' songs. Older teachers may recall such songs as *Bye-Bye Blues, Auf Wiedersen, Arrividerci, Roma, Now is the Hour,* etc. No doubt there are equivalent 'goodbye' songs in the current charts. Pictures of farewell scenes would be a help, too, and the words for goodbye in Spanish (*Adios*), French (*Adieu*), Italian (*Addio*) and any other languages could be displayed for all to see. This could provide an informal talking point with which to begin the Assembly. The main idea to get across is that 'saying goodbye' is part of human life, a sad part, but not one of unrelieved gloom. After discussion of the songs, pictures, words, the leader might start as follows:

Leader 1: Jackie was ten and she had a little fox terrier, called Patch. You can guess why it was called 'Patch'. Jackie loved the dog and the dog loved Jackie. When Jackie came home from school, Patch would be standing on the back of the settee looking for her and he would bark excitedly. As soon as Jackie opened the door Patch would jump up and down with delight. He seemed to know everything that was going on. Sometimes Jackie's mother would say, 'I think Patch can understand English.' Certainly they couldn't say the word 'walk' without Patch going and fetching his lead. If they didn't want Patch to get excited they would have to spell the word — W-A-L-K.

One Friday evening the milkman called for his money. Jackie's mother left the door open while she went for change. Nobody knows what enticed Patch out. It might have been another dog or perhaps a cat. But the next thing was he had gone.

'Never mind,' said Jackie's mother. 'He'll be back tonight.'

But he wasn't. First thing on Saturday morning Jackie and her dad went to the police station.

'Yes,' said the sergeant on duty. 'There was a dog involved in an accident. We took it to the vet's.' They hurried to the vet's. Sure enough there was Patch. 'I have bad news for you,' said the vet, 'I'm afraid Patch is not going to get better.'

The little dog whimpered when he saw Jackie, and Jackie couldn't stop the tears coming into her eyes. Her dad said, 'Come on home, Jackie, and say goodbye to Patch.' It was very, very hard for Jackie as she held the little dog's paw for the last time. 'Goodbye Patch,' she said, 'You've been a good friend to me. Goodbye.'

Leader 2: It's never easy to say goodbye to those we love. But when we say goodbye we can remember that the word means 'God-be-with-you'. And it's the same with the other languages. And one day we pray that we will all, those who have loved each other in this life, meet together again in the next. Just listen to this true story:

43

Reader: Thomas Moore was a great Englishman. He was Lord Chancellor and a great friend of the King. But he followed his conscience and the King had him thrown into prison because he disagreed with him. The King said to him 'Thomas, if you don't agree with me I shall have you executed.'

Thomas had a loving wife and a favourite daughter called Meg. They both came to the prison and tried to persuade him to agree with the King so that he would be released. But Thomas refused. 'I can't do what I believe to be wrong', he said.

On the night before he died, Meg and her mother came to say goodbye. They cried a lot. And Thomas, too, was near to tears but, as they left the prison for the last time, he said 'Don't cry, my love. One day we will meet again merrily in heaven.'

Leader 3: So when we say goodbye to people, even if it seems for the last time, it's only till we meet again in heaven at God's great party for all his friends. The French say 'Au revoir', 'Till I see you again'; the Spanish — 'Hasta luego', 'Till then'. And in English — 'I'll be seeing you' . . . So let's say some prayers about 'goodbye'.

Child 1: We've come to the end of a school year, we ask God to bless those who are leaving our school and whom we may not see again . . .
(Pause)
Lord, in your mercy . . .   . . . **hear our prayer.**

Child 2: We thank God for those who have helped us during the year — teachers, all the staff in the kitchen, traffic warden, the secretary, school caretaker and cleaners.
(Pause)
Lord in your mercy . . .   . . . **hear our prayer.**

Child 3: We pray that we will live well and do what God wants us to do so that one day we will all meet merrily in heaven.
(Pause)
Lord, in your mercy . . .   . . . **hear our prayer.**

Child 4: We pray for all those people who are sad because the people or the animals they love have died. May God comfort them.
(Pause)
Lord, in your mercy . . .   . . . **hear our prayer.**

Child 5: Lastly, we pray that we will all enjoy our holidays and by bringing happiness to others, especially in our own families, we will be happy ourselves.
(Pause)
Lord, in your mercy . . .   . . . **hear our prayer.**

Final song: *Give me joy* [CH 84]